Faith and Prac
at a Quaker School

Faith and Practice at a Quaker School

Be patterns, be examples in all countries, places, islands, nations, wherever you come, that your carriage and life may preach among all sorts of people, and to them: then you will come to walk cheerfully over the world, answering that of God in every one.

George Fox, 1656

"Membra Sumus Corporis Magni"

We are all members of a great body.

© Graham Ralph 2013
© Illustrations, Harvey Herman 2013

ISBN   978 1 904446 49 1

British Library Cataloguing in Publication Data
Graham Ralph 2013
Faith and Practice at a Quaker School

First edition 2014
Second edition 2014

Published and printed by
Quacks Books
7 Grape Lane
Petergate
York YO1 7HU

This document has been written and compiled by Graham Ralph, a teacher at Bootham School, 1980 – 2012.

Illustrations by Harvey Herman, Bootham Old Scholar.

Thanks to the many people who encouraged me to compile this document; to Jenny Bailey who did her best to tidy up the text; to Jonathan Taylor who supported me in taking the sabbatical term to do it and the whole Bootham community who did all my work whilst I was away enjoying myself.

The publication of this book was aided by financial contributions from Bootham School, Quaker Outreach in Yorkshire and the Sessions Book Trust.

Contents

Introduction

A central belief of Quakers is that there is that of God in everyone, and the searching for that within ourselves and others leads us to experience the truth and the light of the world.

Faith and Practice at a Quaker School seeks to describe how Quaker beliefs are put into practice in the everyday life of a school community. It is designed to give everyone who makes up that community (students, staff, parents, committee members, old scholars) and the interested public a description of our faith and our practice and to provide reference points for us to reflect on our role within the school. This *Faith and Practice* may make statements giving advice but will often ask questions about how and why we do things; this is common practice amongst Quakers. "Friends approach queries as a guide to self-examination, using them not as an outward set of rules, but as a framework within which we assess our convictions and examine, clarify, and consider prayerfully the direction of our lives and the life of the community." [1] The responsibility for the answers rests not with someone else but with the individual or the group. The Religious Society of Friends does not have a formal creed.

Faith and Practice at a Quaker School is not a definitive document; it is hoped it will be revised over time as members of the community reflect on their lives. "Only what we have valued and truly made our own, not by assertion but by lives of faithful commitment, can we hand on to the future. Even then, our vision of the truth will again and again be amended." [2]

Meeting for Worship

Silence   *Reflection*

Listening   *Gathered*

Sharing   *Ministry*

As a school community we gather quietly for Meeting for Worship on most mornings of the week. At its best Meeting is a silent waiting and listening to God's truth. For many this might mean simply being quiet and thinking about the day ahead. For some, it is a time to think about each other and the people who mean something to us. Others may find Meeting a time of deeper reflection and contemplation.

All Meetings start and end with a period of silence. In some cases there is an arranged contribution from students or staff; this might be music, a reading, a thought, a film, charity information, a poem. All students and teaching staff are expected to be at Meeting; other staff and visitors are also welcome. It can be a moving experience to have hundreds of people of different ages, sitting in perfect silence listening to the world, to their minds and to their hearts. Any person may be moved to stand and speak during Meeting and we are happy to hear ideas and truths presented by a variety of people in many different ways, for example as a reading, a thought, an observation. We are asked to listen quietly with open minds and respect, even though we are free to discern our own understanding of the Light for ourselves. People of all creeds and none can appreciate this time of reflection.

The experience of sitting together in silence is a daily, practical expression of Membra Sumus Corporis Magni. Many of us have also experienced Meeting with members of the school in other situations, on a hill, in a hotel lobby, under the stars; it is often on these occasions, with others, that the silence can surprise and the spirit can burn even more brightly.

Do I enter the Meeting in an attitude of quiet expectation and openness?

Am I careful not to disturb Meeting by calling attention to myself or by communicating with my friends?

Are you open to new light, from whatever source it may come?
Advices and Queries

Creating time to pause and reflect, creating contemplative time, is a practice that allows people living lives of commitment to the common good to be productive in unexpected, vital and strategic ways.

True worship may be experienced at any time; in any place – alone on the hills or in the busy daily life – we may find God... But this individual experience is not sufficient, and in a meeting held in the Spirit there is a giving and receiving between its members, one helping another with or without words.
Quaker Faith and Practice, 2.11.

Be still and know that I am God.
Psalms 46.10

We listened and heard the silence. We listened and felt the silence. We listened and tasted the silence. We closed our eyes and saw the great silence dwelling within.
Moses Shongo, A Seneca Elder, 1800s

5

...Friends place most emphasis on the manner in which people lead their lives and treat each other. This aspect, as well as the sense of genuine inquiry, allows young people from all religious traditions (or none) to feel comfortable and united during the silence of a Friends school meeting for worship.
Irene McHenry

Lying upon a mound of rocks in a field somewhere near Yealand. Looking at the sky in total silence created an atmosphere of stillness and peace. It was the only meeting I have ever done outside and this made the silence seem so much more pure. The meeting halls of Bootham and Brigflatts may be beautiful but they were beaten by the beauty of having nothing. The darkness cast a spell over the meeting and closed the world in; making our togetherness feel absolute.
Felix Charteris, College Two

the INDIVIDUAL

The Responsibility of the Individual

Respect	Truth
Let Your Life Speak	Light
That of God in Every One	Love

At Bootham we believe that there is that of God in every individual in our community, recognising that 'God' will mean different things to different people. Thus each one of us has a responsibility to discover in others that light and truth which is unique. This responsibility is woven into the everyday through the testimonies that help us reflect on our lives; these are described in the following sections – Truth and Integrity, Equality, Peace and Conflict, Simplicity, Service, Stewardship. These testimonies are the ways in which we recognise the good in each other and how we attempt to put our beliefs into actions. They help us examine our relationship with the other individuals in our community, the environment and society we live in. It follows that respect for life around us should be the norm and that we become who we are by what we do.

As we live in school we all should recognise the responsibility that these testimonies bring and ask each person to examine what the words mean for them. In looking at the responsibility of individuals we need to consider not only how we affect others by our actions but also how we affect ourselves. Our responsibility may be to get involved in school government (Council, the House system, staff committees), or in service, in volunteering, in leadership roles. Some of us will contribute to Bootham by simply being part of the everyday, without having a leading role. In all things it is good to remember - we are what we do.

Let your life speak.
Advices and Queries

Do you reach for the best that is within yourself? Do you look for it in others?

How do I promote a climate of respect among others for considering the ideas of all? [3]

What can we do to make the areas of the school under our care places where friendship, peace and refreshment of spirit can be found? To what extent are we trying to do these things?
North Carolina YM

It is what you do for others that makes you a leader, not the position or the title.
Robert K. Greenleaf

Think it possible that you may be mistaken.
Advices and Queries

Be patterns, be examples in all countries, places, islands, nations, wherever you come, that your carriage and life may preach among all sorts of people, and to them; then you will come to walk cheerfully over the world, answering that of God in every one.
George Fox, 1656

In view of the harm done by the use of alcohol, tobacco and other habit-forming drugs, consider whether you should limit your use of them or refrain from using them altogether. Remember that any use of alcohol or drugs may impair judgement and put both the user and others in danger.
Advices and Queries

Take time to learn about other people's experiences of the Light. While respecting the experiences of others, do not be afraid to say what you have found and what you value. Appreciate that doubt and questioning can also lead to spiritual growth and to a greater awareness of the Light that is in us all.
Advices and Queries

Twenty years from now you will be more disappointed by the things that you didn't do than by the ones you did. So throw off the bowlines. Sail away from the safe harbour. Catch the trade winds in your sails. Explore. Dream. Discover.
Mark Twain

All are especially cautioned against any harshness of tone or manner when administering counsel or reproof, either privately or in meetings. Speak truth with love. Even a seeming harshness may check the beginnings of honest reflection and a lack of sympathy may cause harm where only good was intended.
New York YM

Truth and Integrity

Integrity   Truth

Honesty   Trust

Sincerity   Respect

Quakers use 'Truth' to mean the universal values, principles and convictions about a life led by the spirit inside us. The concept is also seen as demanding honest, simple speech and a refusal to acknowledge the double standards of saying one thing and doing another. In the school it is helpful to be able to assume that each member of the community will feel able to tell the truth in all circumstances. This can be difficult when the decisions we take lead to actions which go wrong. Ultimately it will be best to face up to the issues and eventually to move on.

Truth is an integral part of the Quaker testimony to the Light that is within us all. We can only be true to our innermost self if we are faithful to the truth and honest in our dealings. Truth and integrity are fundamental guiding principles in our own lives and also in our community actions. Quakers believe it is important to tell others about the truth as one sees it. 'Speaking truth to power' for example, means telling people about your concerns and standing up for what you see is right when you think something has gone wrong; this is a vital way of helping the school community work more effectively and encourages respect in our relationships.

Are honesty, truthfulness, and respect for others central in our School community?

Do I try always to speak the truth? [3]

Do I do my work honestly?

How do I deal with dishonesty around me?

Do I hear constructive criticism with humility and without thought of retaliation?

Are you honest with yourself as well as with others?

Do we stand firm when an ethical principle is challenged?

Do we adopt methods of discipline based on trust and mutual support?
Quaker Values in Education

This above all;
To thine own self be true,
And it must follow as the night the day,
Thou canst not then be false to any man.
William Shakespeare, Hamlet

Building community and trust, integrity and caring, a capacity to walk in another's shoes, and cultivating the optimism of the human spirit are even more important goals than imparting knowledge.
Stephen Carey

Take heed, dear Friends, to the promptings of love and truth in your hearts. Trust them as the leadings of God whose Light shows us our darkness and brings us to new life.
Advices and Queries

If pressure is brought upon you to lower your standard of integrity, are you prepared to resist it? Our responsibilities to God and our neighbour may involve us taking unpopular stands. Do not let the desire to be sociable, or the fear of seeming peculiar, determine your decisions.
Advices and Queries

And they gave me the Book, and I took it and was turning to a place that was against swearing, and they took it from me again and bid me say after the clerk. So I told them, if they would prove that Christ and the apostles commanded to swear after they had forbidden it, give us scripture for this, and we would swear. It was Christ's command that we should not swear.
George Fox, 1664

Equality

Fairness   Justice

Understanding   Respect

Diversity

Quakers recognise the equal worth and unique nature of every person. This means working to change the systems that cause injustice and hinder true community. It also means working with people who are suffering from injustice, such as prisoners and asylum seekers.

As a school community we place equality and diversity at the heart of our lives and work. We are committed to promoting equality, whilst recognising that this does not necessarily mean 'treating everyone the same'. Using first names or first and surnames (as is common amongst Quakers) makes us different from many school communities but there are bigger challenges for us in the testimony to equality. We seek to be aware of diversity, to challenge stereotypes, and to meet the individual needs of everyone in order to create and nurture a culture where all people can reach their full potential.

All members of school are important and all relationships can be respectful, easy and enjoyable; when we are relaxed and happy we do our best. We believe that communities which value the good in everyone and respect diversity are essential for a peaceful and just society, where each individual can live without hostility. We assert that achieving such a society requires commitment by us all through the building of good relationships.

Do I see and celebrate the differences among those I meet?[3]

Do I treat every member of the school community with dignity and respect? [3]

Do I speak out against prejudice and discrimination? [3]

Refrain from making prejudiced judgements about the life journeys of others?
Advices and Queries

Does our school provide resources for recruitment to support the opportunities for our community to reflect the broader society in which we live? [3]

How do our school environment and curriculum embrace the concept of equality and create tolerant and open-minded individuals? [3]

Do you respect that of God in everyone though it may be expressed in unfamiliar ways or be difficult to discern? …. Listen patiently and seek the truth that other people's opinions may contain for you.
Advices and Queries

Am I respectful of all people regardless of race, ethnicity, religion, culture, gender, income, age, sexual orientation, physical or learning differences? [3]

Are you alert to practices here and throughout the world which discriminate against people on the basis of who or what they are or because of their beliefs? Bear witness to the humanity of all people, including those who break society's conventions or its laws.
Advices and Queries

Are you working to bring about a just and compassionate society which allows everyone to develop their capacities and fosters the desire to serve?
Advices and Queries

If an employee has a disability, do you try to find work that they can do effectively? Do you make alterations in your working methods and workplace to help them? Do you help them to overcome their own difficulties? [4]

We discovered that it is acceptable to have confused feelings, to be different, to do things our own way. We should not feel guilty when we are wrong, and appreciate that there must be room for mistakes. There are people who want us to be exactly as we are.
Epistle of JYM 1991

There's a Light that was shining when the world began, And a Light that is shining in the heart of man: There's a Light that is shining in the Turk and the Jew, And a Light that is shining, friend, in me and in you.
Sydney Carter

Peace and Conflict

Understanding   Empathy

Conflict Resolution   Trust

Reconciliation   Serenity

Nonviolence

The testimony of peace calls on us to strive for harmony among all people, nations and individuals. If we recognise that every person has a spark of God within, then we will try not to harm one another or to treat others aggressively. If we live in peace, we create community. If we treat all people as if they have the same spark of God in them that we have in ourselves, we practise equality. If we seek to eliminate conditions of inequality in the world, and to value people above possessions, we encourage simplicity. Working for peace can be difficult;- Philip Noel-Baker (Bootham Old Scholar) served in the Friends Ambulance Unit in World War One; this was a non-combative role in which he was decorated for his bravery. Conflict is inevitable but we can learn from others who may disagree with our own view of the world. An empathetic understanding of another's viewpoint is a vital first stage in conflict resolution.

Our peace testimony has helped us to think about and address issues during times of national and world conflict. The school community has met together in Meeting for Worship for a prayerful consideration of what was happening in situations like 9/11, Iraq and the London bombings. Conflict resolution is part of the general studies programme in College Class. Some students and staff voluntarily attend peace vigils at the Minster and at the military base at Menwith Hill. Many students actively support the work of Amnesty International.

Within the school community relationships sometimes fail and behaviour between individuals and groups can go wrong. We believe in Bootham that it is important not to ignore issues:- it is up to everyone to tackle these situations. The innocent victims and the guilty will all need help. Facing up to what has gone wrong, peaceful resolution of conflict and the ability to move on are essential in a caring community.

*Am I committed to an environment that is free of
bullying and other forms of harassment, for all members
of the school community?* [3]

Do I practice peaceful means to work out differences? [3]

*When I am confronted with disagreement or aggression,
how do I respond?* [5]

*Conflict happens, and will continue to happen, even
in the most peaceful of worlds. And that's good – a
world where we all agreed with one another would be
incredibly boring. Our differences help us to learn.*
Quaker Faith and Practice 20.71

*How we deal with our own anger and how we
find peaceful solutions to conflict are important.*
Good Business: Ethics at Work.

*If we are angry we know how wars develop. It
does not matter who's wrong. What matters
is that we care enough to talk to each other.*
Quaker Faith and Practice 20.68

*A good end cannot sanctify evil means; nor must
we ever do evil, that good may come of it....*
Quaker Faith and Practice 24.03

*The peace testimony is about deeds not creeds; not a
form of words but a way of living.*
Quaker Faith and Practice 24.11

*All bloody principles and practices we do utterly deny,
with all outward wars, and strife, and fightings with
outward weapons, for any end, or under any pretence
whatsoever, and this is our testimony to the whole world.*
Declaration to Charles ll, 1660

*The places to begin acquiring the skills and maturity
and generosity to avoid or to resolve conflicts are in our
own homes, our personal relationships, our schools, our
workplaces.*
Yearly Meeting of Aotearoa/New Zealand,1987

*Peace is not a distant goal that we seek, but the means
by which we arrive at that goal.*
Martin Luther King Jr

*Nonviolence is by no means a passive or negative
concept, a simple thou-shalt-not-kill prohibition. It
is a springboard for action, an ideal that must be
transformed into the active pursuit of peace and justice.*
Robert Lawrence Smith [6]

*We are too ready to retaliate, rather than forgive. And
yet we could hurt no man that we believe loves us. Let
us then try what love will do: for if men did once see we
love them, we should soon find they would not harm us.
Force may subdue, but love gains: and he that forgives
first, wins the laurel.*
William Penn 1693

*We may disagree with the views of the politician or
the soldier who opts for a military solution, but we still
respect and cherish the person.*
Quaker Faith and Practice 24.10

Simplicity

Balance

Priority

Clearness

Truth

Appreciation

Many people are concerned about the excesses and unfairness of the consumer society and the unsustainable use of natural resources. It is worth trying to live simply and to give space for those things that really matter: the people around us, the natural world, our spiritual experiences. Quakers believe that it is hard to concentrate on what really matters if our lives are dominated and distracted by worldly ideals. This could be acquiring wealth and possessions, gambling, spending on alcohol and drugs, overly worrying about fashion and appearances, taking too much pride in accomplishments. Early Friends prospered in business and many became quite wealthy; however, a great deal of that wealth was used for the wider benefit of society and especially the dispossessed.

Simplicity involves constantly challenging the way we live and what our true needs are, and especially how our own standard of living is sometimes achieved at the expense of others. We might remember that we are part of a privileged group of people and we have a great deal to give to each other and the world around us. What really matters in school is the community and our relationships and how we might help beyond ourselves. Having a relaxed dress code makes it even more important to consider how clothes can conflict with the search for simplicity; expensive items and designer labels will conflict with this testimony.

When we are investing in our people, our teaching, our buildings, we might look at the right use of resources, what will serve us well over time and what will enable us to focus on what really matters as we educate one another.

*Do I spend resources sensibly, if necessary living with less
so others may have enough?*

*Do I let my possessions and the desire for things dictate
how I live?* [3]

*Do I value persons for their actions and integrity, rather
than their economic background?*

*How does our commitment to simplicity guide us
in being good stewards of our land, buildings, and
resources?* [3]

*How does the school's presentation of itself in
publications and other media speak to the testimony of
simplicity?* [3]

*Drop thy still dews of quietness,
Till all our strivings cease ;
Take from our souls the strain and stress,
And let our ordered lives confess
The beauty of thy peace.*
John Greenleaf Whittier

*Simplicity is not just simple clothes and a simple lifestyle.
It's an organization of the mind that enables you to
sort out the unimportant details that often clutter your
thoughts.*
Sidwell student

I ask for daily bread, but not for wealth, lest I forget the poor.

I ask for strength, but not for power, lest I despise the meek.

I ask for wisdom, but not for learning, lest I scorn the simple.

I ask for a clean name, but not for fame, lest I condemn the lowly.

I ask for peace of mind, but not for idle hours, lest I fail to hearken to the call of duty.

Inazo Nitobe, 1909, Quaker Faith and Practice (20.01)

Try to live simply.   A simple lifestyle freely chosen is a source of strength.   Do not be persuaded into buying what you do not need or cannot afford.   Do you keep yourself informed about the effects your style of living is having on the global economy and environment?
Advices and Queries

Live simply that others may simply live.
Mahatma Ghandhi

Service

Responsibility　　　　Helping

Respect　　　　Leadership

Sharing

With the belief that there is something of God in everyone comes the conviction that we must respond to need wherever it exists, in whomever it exists, not just amongst our friends and peers but wherever we can. When we give of ourselves to help others it helps both the receiver and the giver. [6] Working for others as a service is love made visible and should be undertaken without expectation of reward or thanks.

Friends have taken up service in many ways; they have worked for the abolition of slavery, for prison reform, for the Friends Ambulance Unit, as hospice volunteers, for asylum-seekers and refugees, for the homeless in shelters and soup kitchens. In our community there are many ways in which we can serve. We can help to run our school, through the School Council, the Activities programme, doing duties, organising and looking after social events, taking responsibilities for clubs, societies, younger students, ourselves and each other. There are opportunities to help in the wider world through work with Arclight, the homeless shelter, charity fund raising, supporting initiatives like Crisis at Christmas, Amnesty International.

When we serve we give ourselves the chance to develop in unforeseen ways, in leadership, commitment, empathy, character, compassion, strength, responsibility. After leaving school, many students will take a GAP year at some stage, perhaps choosing to do voluntary work at home or abroad in order to help those less fortunate than themselves; some individuals continue to do this throughout their lives.

Do I willingly engage in community service? [3]

Do I willingly give of my time and energy to committees that serve the health of the community that is Bootham?

Let your life speak.
Advices and Queries

Love thy neighbour as thyself.
Matthew 19.19

Live adventurously. When choices arise, do you take the way that offers the fullest opportunity for the use of your gifts in the service of God and the community?
Advices and Queries

When experience is in the form of service accompanied by sufficient time and structure for reflection, students begin to assume greater responsibility for their own lives and values-based behaviour.
Irene McHenry

A small group of thoughtful, committed citizens can change the world; indeed, it is the only thing that ever has.
Margaret Mead

Let me light my lamp, says the star, and never debate if it will help remove the darkness.
Rabindranath Tagore

Be the change you want to see in the world.
Mahatma Gandhi

Unless someone like you cares a whole awful lot nothing is going to get better.
Dr. Suess

I believe that we are most ourselves when we are connecting with others through service.
Robert Lawrence Smith [6]

Past the seeker as he prayed came the cripple and the beggar and the beaten. And seeing them the Holy One went down into deep prayer and cried, 'Great God, how is it that a loving creator can see such things and yet do nothing about them?' And out of the long silence, God said, 'I did do something. I made you.'
Sufi teaching

The Light is available yesterday, today and to eternity. What is thee doing about it?
Lucretia Mott

The two qualities that are most important to children of today are hope and imagination. Hope to believe they can change the world they live in and imagination to find the ways to do so.
Janet Gilbraith, 1986

STEWARD-
SHIP

Stewardship

Responsibility   Joy

Environment   Conservation

Sustainability

A testimony is not a form of words but an expression of actions characteristic of Friends. New testimonies emerge as the reasons for them and the underlying spiritual basis of action become clarified. Stewardship is one such testimony.

The world is a wonderfully rich resource for our material and spiritual needs. We should treasure it and preserve its capacity to sustain and inspire. That, in turn, calls for a creative responsibility towards the earth we have inherited and for proper sharing. It means seeing that of God in the world around us and being moved by considerations other than commercial gain. Habitats and species are sacrificed to the present, and the needs of others to the wants of the self. It cannot be right to leave the world poorer than we found it, or to consume recklessly in the knowledge that our actions are bound to lead to future tragedy.

Bootham as a community can and does do much to live this testimony:- recycling, raising awareness, sourcing local products, not wasting food, saving energy, building in environmentally friendly ways, teaching sustainability, supporting BEAST/mini-BEAST. But there is always more we as a school and as individuals can do. Membra Sumus Corporis Magni.

Treat the earth well. It was not given to you by your parents, it was loaned to you by your children.

.. all we possess are the gifts of God to us; now in distributing it to others, we act as his stewards....
John Woolman

This we know: the earth does not belong to man, man belongs to the earth. All things are connected like the blood that unites us. We did not weave the web of life, we are merely a strand in it. Whatever we do to the web we do to ourselves.
Chief Seattle of the Suquamish, 1855

Everyone has the right to a standard of living adequate for the health and well-being of himself and of his family, including food, clothing, housing and medical care and necessary social services.
Universal Declaration of Human Rights, 1948,
Article 25.1

True Godliness don't turn men out of the world, but enables them to live better in it, and excites their endeavours to mend it: not to hide their candle under a bushel, but to set it upon a table in a candlestick.
William Penn, 1682

Where we see crisis, we also see opportunity to remake society as a communion of people living sustainably as part of the world.
Susan Seymour, BYM

We do not own the world, and its riches are not ours to dispose of at will. Show a loving consideration for all creatures and seek to maintain the beauty and variety of the world. Work to ensure that our increasing power over nature is used responsibly, with reverence for life.
Advices and Queries

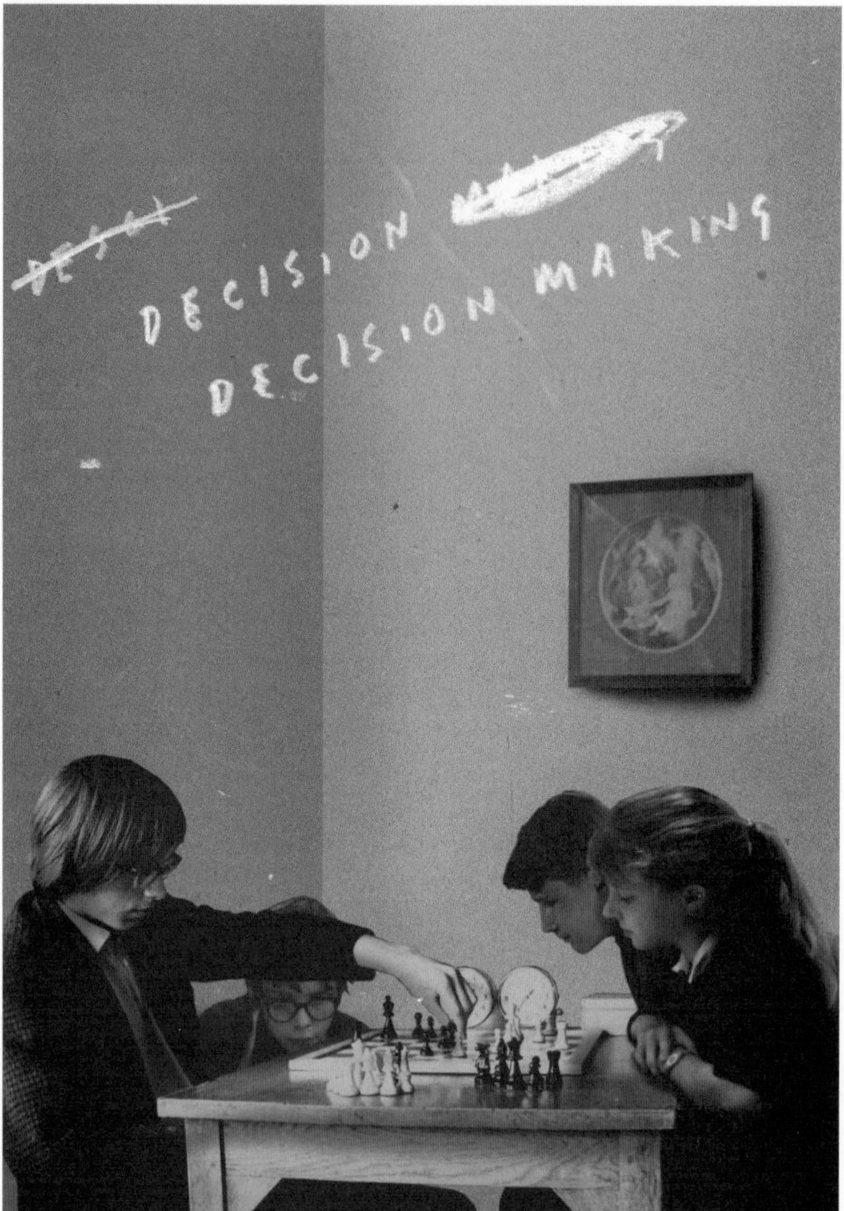
DECISION
DECISION MAKING

Decision Making

Responsibility   Truth

Transparency   Respect

Equality

Quakers are fond of using committees and groups to make decisions because these groups may conduct themselves as 'meetings for worship with a concern for business.' At school many matters are considered in this way. There are the meetings of the School Committee (governors); Strategic Development groups; Staff Meeting; Leadership Meeting; Heads of Department and Heads of Year; School Council; the Nominations Committee for Head Reeves; Departmental Meetings; Old Scholars; Bootham Association Meetings and others. Whatever the meeting there are certain principles which are helpful to their running.

Ideally, all meetings start with a short period of silence. The work of the clerk is vital in the careful guiding of the business process, it should be clear what the decision-making capacity of the group is. No one should dominate discussion and silence may often occur to help consideration. Minutes should record the main points of discussion and all decisions. Minutes are read back in the meeting in order that everyone may confirm their accuracy. Meetings do not usually vote but strive through thoughtful deliberation to find 'a sense of the meeting' where a decision will be made that all can support even if as an individual they may have thought differently. The meeting can be run to encourage coming to decisions that all feel able to support. If people are not comfortable in allowing a decision to be made perhaps the business can be returned to. The Head Reeves are chosen by a nomination committee of students and staff. Discussion centres around the tasks of the role and who would best fit them. These meetings are always confidential.

It is hoped that there can be a spirit of creativity and optimism in most meetings. What can result from the decision making can be enlightened, surprising and invigorating.

Do I listen carefully, deeply, and respectfully to what others have to say? [3]

Do I understand the difference between a decision made by voting and a decision made by consensus that a group has arrived at through seeking the sense of the meeting? [3]

When a decision has been reached do I support it publicly? When necessary do I respect confidentiality? [3]

Do I listen with respect and genuine interest to each person's point of view, whether or not I agree? [3]

Do I actively participate? When I speak do I do it in such a way as not to put others down? [3]

Keep in mind that groups speak through their actions and also through their failure to act. [3]

Listen patiently and seek the truth which other people's opinions may have for you. Avoid hurtful criticism and provocative language. Do not allow the strength of your convictions to betray you into making statements or allegations that are unfair or untrue. Think it possible that you may be mistaken. Advices and Queries

It is no part of Friends' concern for truth that any should be expected to water down a strong conviction or be silent merely for the sake of easy agreement.

Nevertheless we are called on to honour our testimony that to every one is given a measure of the light, and it is in the sharing of knowledge, experience and concern that the way towards unity will be found.
Quaker Faith and Practice, 3.05

The unity we seek depends on the willingness of us all to seek the truth in each other's utterances; on our being open to persuasion; and in the last resort on a willingness to recognise and accept the sense of the meeting as recorded in the minute, knowing that our dissenting views have been heard and considered.
Quaker Faith and Practice, 3.06

Learning

Questioning   Discovery

Creation   Truth-seeking

Teaching   Living Adventurously

A s individuals and as a community, we are committed to helping everyone strive towards, and if possible reach their potential. Working towards realizing the measure of talent we have might also uncover other surprising attributes. Our philosophy should be one of hopeful expectancy in the potential of all members of the community.

A Quaker school should be restlessly searching, experimenting, taking risks; it is change and growth rather than standing still that brings aliveness and even happiness. [6] Bootham can use its small, intimate environment to encourage individual learning opportunities in and out of the classroom. Learning develops most creatively when relationships are based on mutual respect and everyone knows each other as people not just as students and teachers. The school cannot preach kindness and mutual co-operation if its members live and work in ways that accentuate competitive distrust and divisiveness. We believe that we have a responsibility to guide students to voice their own opinions while being receptive to other points of view. [7]

Education includes asking many questions of our teachers, of each other and of ourselves. It is healthy to question assumptions and the status quo. Risking getting things wrong and knowing that we can make mistakes is part of how we learn. Curiosity and enquiry are essential in the Bootham process, encouraging opportunities for collaborative discussion and investigation between all parties.

Watching a million stars shine, feeling the waves break on a volcanic beach, being moved by reading the next line, being shocked by painting that colour... discovering that living adventurously can free the spirit. We all need to experience education, not just receive it. This is what we do.

In what ways am I open to knowledge and to the ideas and beliefs of others. [3]

Do teachers and students get to know and appreciate one another as individuals?

Do we maintain a challenging and vigorous learning environment?

Do we let learning change both our minds and our lives?

How do I help my classes to be meetings for learning? Do I listen with an open mind? [3]

How do I help to create a productive classroom for myself and others?

Think it possible that you may be mistaken.
Advices and Queries

Learning happens most creatively when relationships are based on mutual respect.
Quaker Values in Education

Formal education is only a jumping off point for a lifetime of learning and doing, and what concerns good schools and good teachers is how students apply the learning they acquire to living their lives.
Robert Lawrence Smith [6]

*There is a common pedagogy in Friends Schools...
learning through inquiry, reflection, collaboration,
service, a culture of respect and teachers as partners in
the learning process.*
Irene McHenry

*I feel peace education is about teaching children to
discover that they have the power to change things they
see are wrong and developing the imagination to find
alternative responses to conflict.... If we teach children
to feel their own power we must be ready for them to
criticise the school itself.... The two qualities which
are most important to children of today are hope and
imagination. Hope to believe they can change the world
they live in and imagination to find ways to do so.*
Janet Gilbraith, 1986

*The real voyage of discovery consists not in seeking new
landscapes, but in having new eyes.*
Marcel Proust

*We trust that given the right opportunities children will
grow up into responsible adults capable of making good
choices and of saving the world from disaster.*
Janet Gilbraith, 1986

*It is all too easy to lose your idealism because the outside
world is such a cynical, ruthless place. My school was a
hopeful kind of experience.*
Friends School old scholar

Living in a Caring Community

Welcoming

Acceptance

Interdependence

Trust

Inclusion

Caring

Diversity

Belonging

The idea that there is a light in every human being is the foundation to the responsibilities we have as individuals living in a caring community. There is a fragility and sacredness about each person. The many instances of exploitation, discrimination, injustice and strife in the world call on us to promote harmony, peace and justice. Within the school we take many opportunities to express our care for the disadvantaged of the world. Our work may be through Amnesty International, through BEAST and the push towards Green Flag status, through charity days and our termly charities, working at the homeless shelter, the simple lunches we occasionally have, recycled fashion shows, drama to raise awareness. As individuals we may get sponsorship for charity events, use Gap year opportunities to help those less fortunate, volunteer for leadership in non-timetable days, bring our concerns to Meeting for Worship.

Recognising the uniqueness of each individual and their right to be treated with dignity and respect, we strive to act responsibly in our relationship with one another inside as well as outside our community. In class, with one another in our daily lives, we are asked to show respect no matter what our role. We are encouraged to live peaceably and to resolve differences calmly, through dialogue, and to be honest in our endeavours to reach a positive conclusion. We are always called on to examine our own actions, to be truthful to one another and ourselves.

In a caring community we are encouraged to do our best and to reach our potential; we do not have to be the best. On occasions where we do compete we are encouraged to be better than before, to work hard as a team, to enjoy the camaraderie of achievement together and to enjoy winning fairly with respect for others and for ourselves. In Bootham we deliberately do not rank grades and results from our individual academic achievements; our potential is measured against ourselves not those around us.

*Am I aware that my words as well as my actions
contribute to the climate of the school community?* [3]

*Do you cherish your friendships so that they grow
in depth and understanding and mutual respect?*
Advices and Queries

A person is only a person because of other people.

*Respect the wide diversity among us in our lives
and relationships. Refrain from making prejudiced
judgements about the life journeys of others.*
Advices and Queries

*You never really understand a person until you
consider things from his point of view ... until
you climb into his skin and walk around in it.*
Harper Lee, To Kill a Mockingbird

*It was a blessing to me to come to York in those
days, and there to find it expected on both sides
that the masters were really friends of the boy,
and that the boy could trust the masters to
be just. No two camps, but one united camp.*
Old Scholar, 1850

*I expect to pass through life but once. If therefore,
there be any kindness I can show, or any good thing I
can do to any fellow being, let me do it now, and not
defer or neglect it, as I shall not pass this way again.*
William Penn

A deep reverence for human life is worth more than a thousand executions in the prevention of murder….. The law of capital punishment, while pretending to support this reverence, does in fact tend to destroy it.
John Bright, 1868

Dearly beloved Friends, these things we do not lay upon you as a rule or form to walk by, but that all, with the measure of light which is pure and holy, may be guided; and so in the light walking and abiding, these may be fulfilled in the Spirit, not from the letter, for the letter killeth, but the Spirit giveth life.
From an epistle to 'the brethren in the north' issued by a meeting of elders at Balby, 1656

Write people's virtues on a tablet of stone and their faults on the sand on the seashore.
W.C. Bradley

Some Dates in Bootham History

1823	Founding of the school on Lawrence Street as an all-boys school for sons of Quakers.
1823-5	John Bright; orator, Parliamentarian
1829	John Ford 'Headmaster'. School called 'York Friends Boys' School'.
1834	Natural History Society founded.
1846	The school moves to Bootham.
1847-52	Joseph Rowntree; chocolatier, philanthropist, social Reformer.
1850	Observatory opened.
1856-60	Joshua Rowntree; politician, Quaker activist.
1858-67	Silvanus Thompson; physicist.
1868-71	Edward Grubb; pacifist, social reformer.
1879	Founding of O.Y.S.A (Old York Scholars Association).
1880-86	John Wilhelm Rowntree; chocolatier, Quaker Activist.
1883-88	Seebohm Rowntree; industrialist, sociologist (wrote studies on York poverty).

1891	Bootham first takes boys from non-Quaker families.
1894-8	Lewis Fry Richardson; meteorologist, mathematician, pacifist.
1899	Serious fire to the main building. Arthur Rowntree becomes Headmaster (until 1927).
1902	New library/hall opens, named after John Bright, Parliamentarian and Lawrence St. scholar.
1903-6	Philip Noel-Baker; athlete, diplomat, pacifist, helped found League of Nations.
1914	Penn House sold to school by the Rowntree family. Swimming Pool built.
1915	Bootham School becomes the official name.
1920	Purchase of Rawcliffe Lane playing fields.
1959	Nobel Peace Prize awarded to Philip Noel-Baker
1966	New school Hall opened.
1982	Girls first admitted to school.
1997	Ebor School purchased (becomes Bootham Junior School in 2005)
2002	New Junior School building opened.
2011	Penn House sold.
2014	Arts and Music building opened.

Quaker Terms

Advices and Queries
These are a reminder to Friends of the insights of the Society. They are a series of reflections and promptings to be considered in how they affect us personally and in how we live our lives.

Attender
A person who attends a Local Meeting for worship on a regular basis but is not a member.

Clerk
The person who conducts a meeting for business. They will have ensured that all the information needed for business is gathered for the members of the meeting. The clerk will try to discern the 'sense of the meeting' regarding decisions to be taken forward. The clerk or the assistant clerk will write and read minutes in the meeting after decisions are made. The clerk is the officer of the meeting who assists in its working but is not like the secular 'chair' who may be more dictating of decisions.

Elders
A group of Friends who have a particular responsibility for the spiritual life of the Local Meeting. They will

make sure that Meetings for Worship are rightly held (they will shake hands to end the Meeting), they may organise study groups, they will organise funerals and memorial meetings. Elders are appointed for a maximum of six years.

Faith and Practice

An official edited book of Friends' testimonies, beliefs, reflections and practices usually compiled by a Yearly Meeting of Friends (e.g. Britain Yearly Meeting). The book provides guidance spiritually but will also detail the structure and procedures of the Religious Society of Friends (Quakers). This is where procedures for membership, marriage, business, the structure of the Society, will be found.

Friends Ambulance Unit

An organisation set up in the First World War which enabled Friends (and other conscientious objectors) to serve the injured of all sides in war zones without bearing arms.

I hope so

When the clerk of a meeting reads out a minute of decision he or she will ask "Is that minute acceptable to Friends?" If it is Friends will respond, "I hope so."

Light

This refers to the presence of God in our hearts and lives; a reality that guides us and gives us strength to act. 'Truth' is often used in a similar way.

Local Meeting and Area Meeting

Local Meeting is centred on a meeting house and is made up of local Friends who worship together. Area Meeting is a group of Local Meetings, geographically close, who meet together for business matters (e.g. membership, marriage arrangements).

Meeting for Worship

The gathering of Friends as an act of worship. Friends will gather in silence and may be led to stand and minister. Most often the Meeting is unprogrammed with no arranged structure other than a shaking of hands to close the Meeting. Some Meetings do have more of an arranged structure, for example a Meeting for Worship for Marriage.

Ministry

For a Quaker this term most often applies to standing in a Meeting for Worship and being prompted to express out loud the leadings of the Spirit. One may have little firm idea of what words are going to come out but suddenly, sometimes shaking, you will find yourself on your feet talking.

Minute

The recorded action of a business meeting decision formalising the 'sense of the meeting'. The minute is written in the meeting (a contemporaneous minute), is read aloud and agreed by the assembled members.

Nominations Committees

Groups of Friends who have the work of finding people willing to serve the Society of Friends in various ways, e.g. to be Elders/ Overseers, Clerks etc.

Overseers

A group of Friends from a Local Meeting who have a particular responsibility for the pastoral care of members and attenders of the Meeting. They advise on applications for membership and befriend in order to help when personal difficulties arise. Overseers are appointed for a maximum of six years.

Sense of the Meeting

In reaching decisions in business meetings, Friends do not vote. After full consideration of a matter and allowing for new insights to develop, the collective decision of the Meeting is gathered and expressed by the clerk, in a minute, for the approval of the Meeting. If it is clear that there is an obvious difference of views the matter is held over to a later time.

Testimonies
Convictions based on the experience of Friends that have given direction to their lives.The attempt to put faith into practice. The testimonies do not exist in any rigid, written form; nor are they imposed. All Quakers have to search for the ways in which testimonies can become true for themselves. Some of these testimonies are Truth and Integrity, Equality, Peace, Simplicity, Stewardship.

That of God in Every One
An expression used by George Fox, "… then you will come to walk cheerfully over the world, answering that of God in every one."

Yearly Meeting
The annual gathering of Friends within a particular geographic area. The yearly meeting will come together for worship, business, support, sharing of concerns and friendship. As in Britain Yearly Meeting (BYM).

Quaker Meetings / Membership

Meetings in the York Area

Acomb Local Meeting
Friends' Meeting House, The Green, Acomb, York
YO26 5LR

Harrogate Local Meeting
12a Queen Parade,Harrogate HG1 5PP

Thirsk Local Meeting
24 Kirkgate, Thirsk, YO7 1BL   (01845 524759)

Friargate Local Meeting
Friends' Meeting House, Friargate, York YO1 9RL
(01904 624065)

New Earswick Local Meeting
White Rose Avenue, New Earswick, York YO32 4AD

More information about Quakers can be found at:-
www.yorkquakers.org.uk
www.quaker.org.uk

The Religious Society of Friends

The Religious Society of Friends, called Quakers, formed as a movement in the mid-1600s. It has its roots in an area of Lancashire and the southern Lake District often called '1652 Country'. George Fox, a travelling charismatic preacher was mainly responsible for the establishment of the Society of Friends. There are today approximately 300,000 Quakers worldwide; 25,000 people worship at Meetings every Sunday in Britain.

Generally people apply for membership after several years of being familiar with Friends ways and beliefs; they may wish to show their commitment to Friends and their recognition that this is their spiritual home. The applicant would probably make their intention known to Friends in the Local Meeting. A letter of application is made to the Clerk of the Area Meeting and two Friends (one of whom is well known to the applicant) are appointed to visit. This is a conversation, possibly over an evening, to share the beliefs and understandings of the applicant. A short report of the visit is made to Area Meeting and Friends are most likely to accept the membership at the next Area Business Meeting.

References

A Light That Is Shining: An introduction to the Quakers. Harvey Gillman.

A Quaker Book of Wisdom. Robert Lawrence Smith. [6]

Advices and Queries for Friends School Community Life: Friends Council on Education.

Bootham Leavers Year Book 2011. Felix Charteris.

Faith and Practice, Friends School of Baltimore. [3]

Faith and Practice, Philadelphia Yearly Meeting [1]

Faith and Practice, Germantown Friends School, Philadelphia. [5]

Good Business: Ethics at Work. [4]

Quaker Faith and Practice, Britain Yearly Meeting. [2]

Quaker Values, Leighton Park School.[11]

Quaker Values in Education.

Readings on Quaker Pedagogy. Irene McHenry, Jane Fremon, Nancy Starmer, J.Harry Hammond.

Testimonies, Sidwell Friends School, Washington D.C.

The Meaning of Simplicity. Mike Shaw.

The Peculiar Mission of a Quaker School. Douglas Heath. Pendle Hill, 1982.

The Quaker Testimonies. QPSW.

Those Years. Arthur Rowntree.